Carlisle Castle

Henry Summerson

Introduction

Some English castles evoke romantic images of the Middle Ages, inviting the visitor to think of noble knights keeping watch from gorgeous pinnacles from which they will ride out in times of war to perform deeds of chivalry. Carlisle Castle is emphatically not one of these. Its red sandstone walls keep a generally low profile, broken only by the massive outline of the keep, and the whole castle wears a dour and pugnacious look, as if ready for anything an attacker can throw at it. It is a look it has worn for nearly 900 years, for, unlike most castles, it never either fell into ruin or underwent conversion from a fortress into a stately home, but was still occupied by soldiers within living memory. Each century altered or added to what it had inherited from its predecessor. Thus, a castle which, in its 12th-century beginnings, was as much a symbol of royal prestige as a fortress, became the mighty border stronghold against the Scots of the later Middle Ages. The base from which the March wardens of the Tudors patrolled an unruly frontier had by the early 18th century become a comfortable retirement home for army pensioners. Last of all, and most unexpectedly, the government's need to keep troops at Carlisle in order to control political unrest in the early 19th century led to a prolonged building programme that resulted in many old structures being renovated and several new ones being put up. As a result, what the visitor sees today is an architectural medley, in which it is possible to see how a medieval framework was continually adapted to meet the different needs of succeeding generations. It is in this process of continual change and development that much of the castle's fascination lies.

Tour

Carlisle Castle represents nine centuries of military and royal activity near the Anglo-Scottish border. The tour explores the different architectural features of the site, revealing how the castle functioned at various times as a fortress, residence, military training centre and prison. It describes fascinating features, such as the so-called prisoners' carvings, and explains how the castle has evolved from a medieval stronghold into the complex monument we see today.

FOLLOWING THE TOUR

The castle's curtain wall encloses a large outer ward where the buildings are still in use. The oldest surviving parts within the curtain walls are the gatehouse at the entrance, the half-moon battery, and the buildings of the inner ward, which include the keep and the walkway. It is these parts of the castle that are included in the tour. The numbers beside the headings highlight key points on the tour route, and correspond with the small numbered plans in the margins. The different parts of the castle are also labelled on the orientation view on the inside front cover.

Left: Depot staff and soldiers of the Border Regiment at the castle gate, 28 October 1911, the 100th anniversary of the British victory over France at the battle of Arroyo dos Molinos in the Peninsular War
Below: A similar view of the outer gatehouse today

Facing page: Carving of a head wearing an elaborate helmet typical of about 1480. Immediately below it is a much cruder carving of a stag. These carvings are conserved on the second floor of the keep

◼ OUTER GATEHOUSE

The outer gatehouse is sometimes referred to as De Ireby's Tower, presumably taking its name from William de Ireby, an important royal official active in Cumberland in the early 13th century. It encapsulates much of the history and complexity of the castle. Like every other building, it has served many purposes over the centuries, and has accordingly been much rebuilt, patched and added to. Its oldest parts probably date from the 1160s, but substantial changes were made by the architect John Lewyn between 1378 and 1383. The front line of the castle's defences, it was also the sheriff of Cumberland's office, and contained his 'exchequer', where the county revenues were paid. In later centuries it became a barracks (in 1841 it housed 29 men), and then, after the beds were removed, it served as the sergeants' mess, though it was inconveniently dark and poky – a report of 1938 observed that 'if they [the NCOs] were not a sober lot they would break their necks on the stairs'.

A tour of the gatehouse is best started in the front room at ground level. The small window in its east wall is modern, but the windows to the south and west, though recent in design, replaced earlier openings from which the gatekeeper could watch the approaches to the castle and keep an eye on the curtain wall. Basic comforts were provided by a fireplace in the south wall and a latrine in the south-west corner. Under the floor is what could have been either a cellar or a prison – perhaps it served both purposes as the need arose. The space behind this room, now the ticket office and shop, was originally two rooms, probably an anteroom with a chamber behind for an officer serving the grander rooms upstairs. This chamber, too, has a fireplace and a latrine – the entrance to it is visible to the right of the window in the west wall.

First Floor

The stairs at the back lead up to a suite of rooms on the first floor. Although it has been argued that these were intended to accommodate the warden of the March, it is unlikely that a man of his importance would willingly have occupied a space so small, and probably they housed the sheriff, whose offices also formed part of the gatehouse. What now looks like a single large room was originally divided in two by a screen running across from near the stairhead. This created a service

Above: The outer gatehouse, viewed from outside the curtain walls. The front line of the castle's defences, this impressive entrance was largely rebuilt in the late 14th century

Right: This third-century Roman altar was used as a lintel over the door leading from the withdrawing chamber to a spiral staircase. It was dedicated by a Syrian soldier serving in the 20th legion – service in the Roman army often involved travelling a long way from home

area (with its own fireplace, close to the stairway) for the kitchen, from which food could then be brought into what was in effect a separate hall.

Kitchen

The pointed arch in the south wall (the square-headed door next to it is a later addition) gives access to the kitchen. It contained two large fireplaces, one in the east wall, with a small storage space cut in the wall next to it, and the other in the south – a hole which once supported a pot-hanger can be seen in the arch over the latter. In the lower levels of the west wall, there are traces of a sink. There is no well in the gatehouse, however, and all the water used in this kitchen had to be brought in from outside. The door in the south-east corner of the kitchen is a later addition, perhaps made when the gatehouse was fortified against 'radicals' in 1819. No doubt it came in useful later, when a beer garden for the sergeants' mess was laid out on the barbican outside.

Hall

Back in the hall, a table and chairs have been placed, as they were centuries ago, where the medieval occupant of the gatehouse and his household sat and ate, warmed from the large fireplace whose remains can be seen in the south wall. The three windows in the hall are either enlargements of smaller originals or the product of later alterations, and in the Middle Ages the room must have been cold, with the gate passage immediately beneath it, and gloomy in winter and on overcast days. It could also have been noisy, thanks to the working of the portcullis, the top of which is visible in the thickness of the wall under the south-facing window. The portcullis was probably operated from the battlement over the gateway and barbican. Also in the north wall of the hall is a doorway giving access to a stairway. This leads up to a recent reconstruction of the chamber that was formerly set above the service area – it might well have been intended to accommodate servants. It has what is probably a later fireplace in its south wall, while a door in its west wall gives access to the south curtain wall. The doorway to the left of the fireplace once opened into another chamber above the kitchen.

Withdrawing Chamber

The room beyond the hall which contains a large bed was a withdrawing chamber to which residents retired for privacy and comfort. It acted as both sitting room and bedroom. The door connecting it to the hall was originally at the north end of the wall separating the two rooms, but access is now through a passage at the opposite end of the wall. In the south wall of this passage is a door onto the barbican. In the withdrawing chamber are the remains of two fireplaces: the first, in the south wall near the way into the room, has now been turned into an alcove; the second, dating from the 16th century and largely made of brick, is set in the east wall, where it replaced a small window. Next to the first fireplace is a passage leading to a latrine, which was later turned into a doorway onto the outer battlements. In the north-west corner of the withdrawing chamber is a doorway leading to a spiral staircase. It is kept locked, but is of interest for its original lintel, now standing on the floor nearby. It formed part of a Roman altarpiece, and the remains of its inscription show that it was dedicated to the gods Jupiter, Juno, Minerva, Mars and Victory by a tribune of the 20th legion, who described himself as 'a Syrian from Nicopolis in the province of Thrace'.

OUTER GATEHOUSE:
SECTION AND PLANS

Section

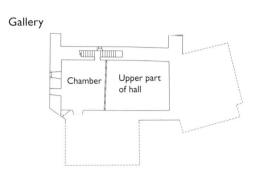

Gallery

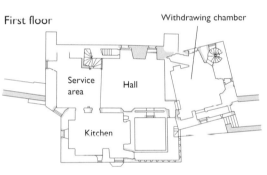

First floor

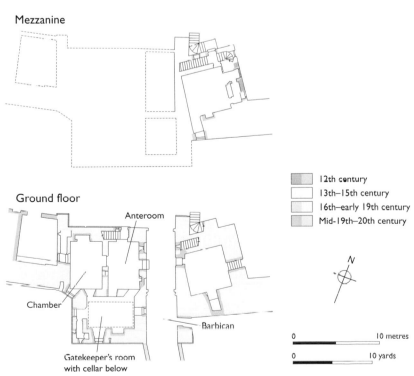

Mezzanine

Ground floor

■ 12th century
□ 13th–15th century
□ 16th–early 19th century
■ Mid-19th–20th century

0 ___ 10 metres
0 ___ 10 yards

7

Below: Depot staff and soldiers of the Border Regiment on parade in the outer ward on a wet day in 1928. The half-moon battery (excavated only ten years earlier), Captain's Tower, and part of the keep are visible in the background

☑ OUTER WARD

The visitor who looks across the asphalt parade ground, with its parked cars and patches of lawn, to the buildings in front of the outer walls, might reasonably wonder if this was a medieval castle at all. In the Middle Ages this was mostly open ground, with just a few mainly wooden structures dotted around it. One of these was the 'great hall for the king's household' which was put up in the outer ward when Edward I stayed in Carlisle in 1307, and probably accommodated the parliament that was held in the city in that year. As late as the 1820s, the parade ground was covered with grass, and provided grazing for cows and sheep.

The impressive two- and three-storey brick buildings visible today were erected in the 19th and 20th centuries, when the castle was a regimental depot designed to accommodate hundreds of soldiers. They are still in use today, and are therefore not open to the public. Between 1873 and 1959 the castle was the home of what became the Border Regiment, and apart from the one in the south-west corner – the officers' mess, put up in 1876 – all these structures bear the names of 19th- and 20th-century battles in which the Border Regiment or its forerunners played a prominent part: Ypres, Gallipoli, Arroyo (the former regimental gym is just visible behind it), Arnhem and finally Alma, the most recent addition to the castle complex, which was built in the early 1930s.

☑ HALF-MOON BATTERY

It is only on the east side of the parade ground that evidence for the castle's earlier history becomes clearly visible. Between a ditch and the wall and gatehouse of the inner ward stand the remains of the half-moon battery, built in the 1540s when the defences of Carlisle, castle and city alike, were being overhauled. This semicircular structure provided extra protection to the approaches to the inner ward, the nerve centre of the castle. It had walls on each side of it above the ditch, and originally stood much higher than it does now. At ground level there was a stone parapet with three openings for cannon, and it was also defended below. A steep flight of stairs leads down into the lower levels of the battery. Here there is a semicircular gallery with windows

Left: An engraving of 1813 by Luke Clennell showing the Captain's Tower and half-moon battery to the left and the outer gatehouse in the background. The neglected state of the walls and overgrown condition of the outer ward are all too obvious

Below: The half-moon battery and the Captain's Tower behind. The battery originally stood high enough to enable soldiers to shoot out over the outer ward, but was levelled in the 19th century when the parade ground was created and the moat filled in

for 11 soldiers (and one more on each of the two stairs). They would originally have been able to shoot straight out over the outer ward – its ground level was raised by several feet when the parade ground was laid out in the 1830s. There are three blocked vents in the ceiling which once provided outlets for gunpowder smoke – a serious nuisance until the invention of smokeless powder in the late 19th century.

4 CAPTAIN'S TOWER

Immediately behind the half-moon battery stands the Captain's Tower, which as its name suggests was the residence of the officer responsible for the day-to-day running of the castle as a military unit. The tower projects well forward, enabling its defenders to command the walls on either side of it. The bases of those walls are chamfered, sloping outwards, to provide extra protection against attack by mining and battering. The gatehouse is essentially a product of the late 12th century, when the inner ward was created as a separate unit within the castle, but like all the other buildings it was much altered later. Although it is

9

CAPTAIN'S TOWER: SECTION AND PLANS

Section

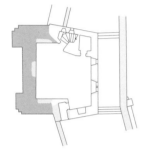

Second floor

First floor

Ground floor

	12th century
	13th–15th century
	16th–early 19th century
	Mid-19th–20th century

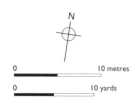

0 —————— 10 metres
0 —————— 10 yards

not always possible to say exactly when changes were made, the grey stone probably marks the building's earliest stages, while the dark red sandstone reflects later additions and alterations.

The arch of the gatehouse's entrance-passage is framed by a higher, older one, with a single slit window above it. The joist-holes cutting through the top of the earlier arch probably date from the early 19th century, when the castle was put in a state of defence out of fear that it would be attacked by a revolutionary mob (see pages 36–8). It is not known when the three blocked rectangles were cut through. The inner moat, which ran rather closer to the tower before the half-moon battery was constructed, was crossed by a drawbridge, which was worked from the gatehouse and when raised probably rested against an upright framework placed on the edge of the ditch. The entrance to the gatehouse itself could be barred by gates, while at the other end of the passage there was a portcullis (worked from a first-floor chamber), followed by another pair of gates – you can see the portcullis grooves, and then the hinges of the gates. Any attacker who penetrated the gate passage could also be attacked from above, with missiles fired through holes whose outlines are still visible. The peacetime visitor could be scrutinized from the guardroom on the south side of the passage.

Captain's Tower from the Inner Ward

Up to this point the gatehouse seems entirely functional and defensive. But seen from within the inner ward – the medieval castle's principal residential area – it takes on a more ornamental appearance. The east end of the gate-passage was decorated with a finely cut band of tracery (which may include a carving of the coat of arms of the Neville family), with an elegant triple window above it, and graceful pilasters on either side; the one on the left survives, though broken off a few feet above the ground, the other was destroyed by later works, perhaps when the topmost arch was inserted. This was made necessary by the reordering of the whole inner ward in the 1540s, enabling heavy guns to be set on its walls and moved around its battlements. The new arch made it possible for cannon to be moved directly from one side of the Captain's Tower to the other.

5 INNER WARD

On the north side of the inner ward is the old militia store (see below), which houses an exhibition on the history of Carlisle Castle. The buildings here bear the marks of their adaptation to accommodate soldiers in the 19th century, as do the rooms inside the Captain's Tower – 25 men were packed into this building in 1827. Until the early 19th century the north wall of the inner ward was lined by medieval buildings forming a suite originally intended for royal occupation, the so-called 'palace' built on the orders of Edward I (r. 1272–1307.). But from about 1806 these were either demolished and replaced or substantially rebuilt. Immediately to the left of the gatehouse are three garage-like hollows cut into the thickness of the wall next to the gatehouse – 16th-century storage spaces, or casemates. Then comes the powder magazine, built in 1827 to hold up to 320 barrels of gunpowder. Next to it stands the militia store of 1881, which distributed uniforms and supplies to what was in effect the army reserve – part-time soldiers who needed them during their annual training periods.

'Palace'

The powder magazine and militia store occupy the site of the great hall of the 'palace'. At the east end of the hall stood the great chamber; its surviving shell is all that remains of the medieval 'palace'. From 1973–2014 it was occupied by the King's Own Royal Border Regiment Museum.

Facing page: The octagonal stair turret that once gave access to the great chamber and Queen Mary's Tower

Left: Detail from a watercolour of about 1810 by Luke Clennell, showing the Captain's Tower from the inner ward. Like Queen Mary's Tower, the fine tracery above the gateway is a rare example of 14th-century decoration in the castle

Below: Watercolour of about 1790 by Robert Carlyle, showing buildings of the medieval palace against the north wall of the inner ward. The hall is to the left; the great chamber at that time still had its external stair and first-floor porch

Right: Wash drawing of
Queen Mary's Tower by
J M W Turner, 1797. The two
windows on the upper floor
provided light for the
chamber which Mary, queen
of Scots, was believed to
have occupied when she
stayed in the castle. It was
demolished in 1835

The outlines of earlier doors and windows on its otherwise regular Georgian-style exterior show that it has often been altered. A watercolour from about 1790 (see page 11) reveals that it was originally entered by a stair leading up to a porch on the first floor, which had an undercroft, containing a kitchen and buttery, beneath it. The same picture shows that it then still had fine late-medieval windows. Inside, a handsome 16th-century fireplace survives on the first floor. After centuries of neglect it became the officers' mess in the early 19th century, and afterwards the quartermaster's stores. The chamber's importance and architectural quality is most striking at its east end, where two sides of a richly carved octagonal stair turret survive (more of it is visible inside). There is elegant blank arcading above the door, set between pilasters terminating in carved heads.

Queen Mary's Tower

The turret gave access both to the chamber and to a now vanished tower that stood in the south-east corner of the ward, known successively as the New Tower, the Warden's Tower, and finally Queen Mary's Tower, after its most famous occupant, Mary, queen of Scots, who spent some weeks in it after arriving in England in 1568.

When built in 1308, the two-storey tower occupied one of the oldest parts of the castle, the site of the original entrance in the east wall, where another late 18th-century watercolour shows a blocked-up round arch. It was said to have had a window from which Mary could look towards Scotland – this is confirmed by a description of the 1830s of 'a spacious room called the queen's bedchamber lighted by two windows facing to the south and one to the north' on the first floor. The same report described the tower as 'in a richer style of architecture than the other parts of the castle', making its loss all the sadder. In 1819 it was turned into barracks, accommodating 38 men. But the resulting hard usage was too much for a structure which had been neglected for centuries, and in 1835 it was demolished when on the verge of collapse. Now only a few foundations can be seen in the angle where the tower stood.

Dacre Postern

Turning back along the south curtain wall towards the keep, the so-called Dacre postern, named from the stone plaque outside carved with the Dacre arms of three scallops, can be seen in the

Mary, Queen of Scots, at Carlisle

A famous prisoner in Carlisle Castle was Mary, queen of Scots. Defeated by rebellious subjects in May 1568, she fled to England and was brought to Carlisle, where she was housed in what was then known as the Warden's Tower, in the south-east corner of the inner ward. Her numerous attendants included the lady-in-waiting who prepared her hair, so skilfully that 'every other day-lighte she hath a new devyce of head dressing'. Mary borrowed money from city merchants to help her keep up a suitably royal appearance, but the cost of maintaining her little court fell principally on Queen Elizabeth, who paid an average of £56 a week for commodities such as meat, fish, spices, biscuits, butter, peat for heating and Gascon wine. Sir Francis Knollys, who had been appointed to keep an eye on the Scottish queen, went in constant fear that she would escape. He allowed her to walk on the grass in front of the castle – thereafter known as 'the lady's walk' – and to watch members of her entourage playing football. But when she went out on horseback to hunt a hare, 'she galloping so fast upon every occasion', he put his foot down and said that this could not happen again. Eventually the Scottish queen was persuaded to leave for Bolton Castle in Yorkshire, the home of the March warden, Lord Scrope, who had himself been forced to keep watch at Carlisle at night in case Mary tried to escape. Four carriages, 20 packhorses and 23 riding horses were needed to convey her, her retinue, and her belongings.

Sir Francis Knollys allowed Mary to walk on the grass in front of the castle, and to watch members of her entourage playing football

Left: Mary, queen of Scots, a miniature portrait painted by Nicholas Hilliard (1542–87) in about 1578

Right: The plaque and inscription of 1577 on the wall of the governor's range next to the keep conveys the message that the castle both serves and is dependent upon the Crown. These are replicas; the original stones can be seen in Cumbria's Museum of Military Life

Below right: The east elevation of the keep, as seen from near the south-east angle of the walkway round the inner ward

Overleaf: The north elevation of the keep, showing the stepped ramp giving access to the walkway

wall itself. Most likely it was made while Thomas, second Lord Dacre, was warden of the West March in the years around 1500. The little stone shed, originally a 19th-century storekeeper's office, was used for testing gas masks during the Second World War.

Governor's Range

The wall projecting from the keep was part of the large 16th-century building known as the governor's range. Set into its wall is the replica of a plaque and inscription recording that in 1577: *Sumptibus hoc fecit propriis opus Elizabetha Regina occiduas Dominus Scroop dum regit oras* – 'Queen Elizabeth carried out this work at her own expense while Lord Scrope rules the West Marches'. The coat of arms, initials and motto underline an important point about the whole castle, that it existed to serve the needs and policy of the Crown, upon which it depended entirely for its maintenance and development.

The governor's range filled the space between Queen Mary's Tower and the keep. It was originally only two storeys high, but was raised by two more floors in the 18th century – the surviving stretch of wall gives at least a partial idea of its height. It might well have owed its name to its occupation during the reign of King Charles II by Sir Philip Musgrave, the governor of Carlisle, who probably died there in 1678. An inventory taken at his death records that he slept

in a room containing a curtained bed with two feather mattresses, five chairs and stools, six cushions, hangings, a screen and a looking glass. The range later fell into decay, and having been described in 1811 as 'unoccupied and in a state of ruin', it was almost entirely demolished a year later.

6 KEEP

The keep, or great tower, is the largest and most impressive part of the castle – it is some 21 metres (69 feet) high. In a complex full of buildings that have been reworked, rebuilt, or even demolished altogether, one might suppose that at least this huge structure, which has dominated the northern approaches to Carlisle for nearly nine centuries, had survived the years without being too badly knocked about. Nothing, however, could be further from the truth. It was originally even higher, until the roof level was lowered in the 16th century to make the top a more effective gun emplacement, while the interior has been endlessly adapted to meet the needs of successive generations of occupants.

It is not always easy to say what those needs were. Great towers were not only defensive strongholds, they were also striking expressions of their builders' authority. 12th-century writers often call them 'donjons', a word derived from the Latin *dominium* ('lordship'). A donjon both made an emphatic statement of power, and provided a setting within which that power was wielded.

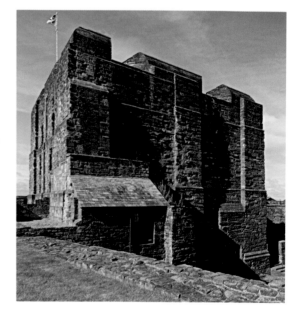

RECONSTRUCTION DRAWING OF
CARLISLE CASTLE IN ABOUT 1400

KEY

1 Outer gatehouse
2 Captain's Tower
3 Inner ward
4 Keep
5 New Tower (later
   Queen Mary's Tower)
6 Kitchen
7 Great hall
8 Great chamber
9 Curtain wall
10 Outer ward

The keep is now entered at ground level, through a 16th-century doorway that probably replaced an early 12th-century original, and to which a portcullis operated from a chamber above gave added protection. But the visible foundations on either side of the doorway show that there was a change of plan here at an early date. They mark the position of a forebuilding, a structure found in a number of 12th-century castles to heighten security and make a more impressive entrance, and which housed an imposing external stairway giving access to the first floor.

Probably the forebuilding was a short-lived change to the initial plan, one tempting to associate with the period between 1135 and 1157, when Carlisle was under Scottish occupation. David I financed building works at Carlisle, which became a centre for the government of his realm and where he died. The forebuilding was set in front of what was at first, and later became again, the main entrance to the keep. It gave access (as today) to a straight stair cut in the thickness of the wall. This leads up to a lobby that holds the blocked-up doorway that once led from the forebuilding into the keep (and later also to the governor's range outside). On the other side of the lobby is the entrance to the keep's first floor.

First Floor

Except perhaps at ground level, the spine wall that now divides every floor was probably inserted in the 16th century to support the weight of heavy guns. There is no clear evidence for such a wall in earlier centuries, even though buildings of similar dimensions often contained one. It was therefore probably within a single large space, possibly divided by screens, that the king – whether he was Henry I or David I – received visitors and petitioners in appropriate state. There is a much altered fireplace in the east wall, and a chamber in the corner from which the portcullis was operated after the forebuilding was abandoned. Another door in the north wall gives access to a chamber from which water could be drawn up from the castle well (this can be seen from outside), as well as to another room whose purpose is unknown.

The door in the middle of the central wall gives access to a second large chamber basically

KEEP: SECTION AND PLANS

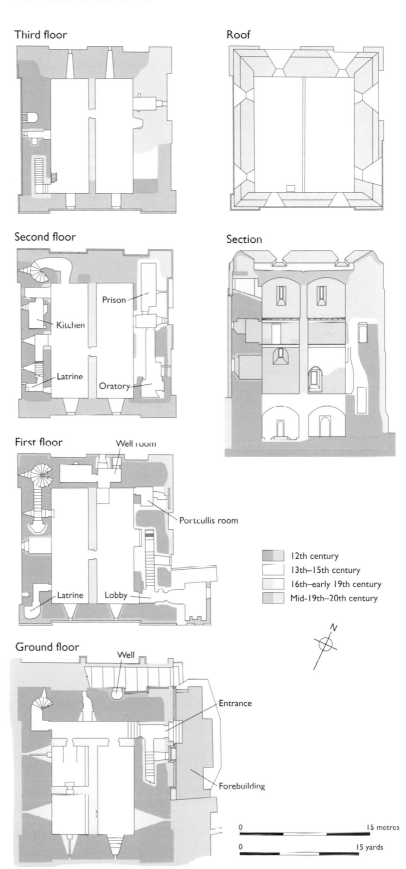

Third floor

Roof

Second floor

Prison

Kitchen

Latrine

Oratory

Section

First floor

Well room

Portcullis room

Latrine

Lobby

12th century
13th–15th century
16th–early 19th century
Mid-19th–20th century

Ground floor

Well

Entrance

Forebuilding

N

0   15 metres

0   15 yards

identical with the first. In the left-hand corner a doorway leads to a latrine – the dog-leg passage gave privacy and helped to reduce the smell. The handsome central window, like much else on this floor, has been heavily restored. In the Middle Ages, for as long as these rooms remained in residential or ceremonial use, the walls would have been plastered, and then either painted or covered with hangings. The disappearance of the plaster at least makes it possible to see how much the walls have been cut about. Whatever its symbolic importance as an emblem of royal power, for much of its history the keep was more likely to contain things – military stores and stockpiles of food and drink – than people. Then in the early 19th century it was pressed into service as barracks, with two rooms (probably those on the first floor) being adapted in 1834 to provide accommodation for 34 soldiers. Perhaps it was to provide them with extra light that an old window in the north wall was reopened.

Second Floor

The second floor, which originally constituted the keep's top storey, is reached through a door in the first floor's right-hand corner, where a short stairway down connects to a spiral stair coming up from below. This originally probably contained living quarters. On the right of the stairhead is a

rectangular chamber which was the service room for the kitchen which opens off its left-hand side – the fireplace survives in its end wall. Further along the main room's west wall is a doorway that now opens onto the stairway up to the third floor, but originally led to another latrine – another doorway on the other side of the stair gives access to it. The central wall is rather eccentrically pierced by a doorway which has a pointed arch on one side and a flat top on the other. Facing it in the chamber beyond is a blocked up fireplace, to the left of which can seen one of the castle's most remarkable features, the so-called prisoners' carvings. There is no access through this door to the chambers beyond, one of which (that to the right) might have been the oratory where David I died in 1153.

Third Floor

On the third floor are two plain, brick-vaulted chambers, inserted in the 16th century. They were probably intended to serve as a gunpowder store for the cannon that were now placed upon the roof. If so, the results were unfortunate, for in about 1547 the magazine blew up, leaving the whole keep 'marvellous cracked'. The damage was not repaired for the best part of a century. The roof of the keep is closed to visitors.

Ground Floor

The best way back to ground level is by the stairs that led up from the first floor, then continuing down by the spiral staircase, which leads to a narrow passage that ends in a short flight of stairs up to the entrance. Off this passage are two large

The Prisoners' Carvings

On the second floor of the keep is a doorway to a short passage (now protected by glass doors) opening onto a room to either side – the oak door of one hangs on the wall nearby. Along this short passage are numerous carvings: some are true graffiti, little more than scratches, but others are skilfully carved, and may all be the work of a single hand. They are often attributed to prisoners, but this is questionable, as they appear only in this lobby-like space, which seems unlikely to have been used as a cell. The rooms to either side may have been, however, so it is possible the carvings were made by bored guards on duty here. It is even possible they were made by a resident priest (there was a chapel in the 'palace' complex). Their date is more certain: the heraldry, armour and dress all point to about 1480, when Richard, duke of Gloucester (later Richard III) was Warden of the March. There are three carvings of his badge, the boar, as well as the badges of the Dacres (the scallop), and the Percys (the fetterlock), who were his adjutants. Religion is represented by a carving of St George and the dragon, several crucifixes, Christ on the cross between two saints, the IHS monogram of the sacred name of Jesus, and a figure with a wheel who is probably St Katherine. Two carvings show a mermaid holding a mirror, a traditional symbol of vanity also found on the choir stalls of Carlisle Cathedral. Others may have been no more than fantasies – not always agreeable ones, since as well as strange birds and beasts (perhaps scenes from folklore) there is a naked woman threatened with spears.

The upper rooms of the keep are not known to have been used as a gaol, and members of the garrison or a priest seem just as likely to be responsible for these carvings

Above: Carving of a naked woman attacked with spears
Left: The true authorship of the carvings is not known, but they date from about 1480. The boar, badge of Richard III, is at the bottom right. The Percy fetterlock (an inverted 'D' shape) is left of the boar, while the fish on the far left, above another, smaller, boar, probably represent dolphins, associated with the Greystokes, a powerful northern family whose heiress married Thomas, second Lord Dacre in 1487

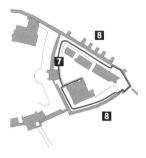

Right: The inner ward's walkway was widened and strengthened in the mid-16th century to take the weight of cannon. These two 24-pounders are of a later date, but still give a fair idea of the size of the artillery that the castle now had to accommodate

vaulted chambers, the first of them divided into two by a cross-wall with a door through it. All the architecture here is plain and functional. These rooms are sometimes referred to as dungeons, but, though they might occasionally have held prisoners, their basic purpose was to hold stores, in particular bulky and heavy items such as barrels of beer that might endanger the floors at higher levels. In 1640, the two bottom floors of the keep were said to have been reserved for 'provision that is casked'.

⏹ WALKWAY OF THE INNER WARD

A stepped ramp from the keep leads up to the walkway round the walls of the inner ward. The ramp was created to carry guns up to the walkway, which in turn was broadened and reinforced, with buttresses outside and an earthen rampart within a retaining wall inside, enabling cannon to be moved around on it. It also makes it possible to see the well in the north face of the keep. It is about 21 metres deep, and, as the inner ward's only source of water when the gates were closed, was accessible from both outside and inside the keep. Turning left at the top of the ramp and then walking round will give good views over the city, and also reveal some of the architectural detail both of the keep and of the buildings lining the north wall, especially the octagonal turret on the corner of the regimental museum. In the corner where Queen Mary's Tower once stood, it

is possible to see that the battlement has been perforated by narrow slits suitable for soldiers holding rifles, reflecting the fears of the 1830s, when the castle was thought to be in danger of attack by rebels and rioters. Further on there are bigger and older embrasures for cannon, made when Scottish invasion remained a possibility. Two 24-pounders still stand on the walkway. The arch at the back of the Captain's Tower makes it possible to complete a circuit before returning to ground level.

⏹ OUTSIDE THE CASTLE GATE

When leaving the castle, it is worth looking at the outside of the outer gatehouse. Its eastern and western sections are not properly aligned, for whereas the western parts are set straight along the moat, its eastern sections, behind the outworks, or barbican, over the passage, slant perceptibly away from it. This is probably due to a change of plan while the gatehouse was being built, which led to the buildings on the east side of the gate passage retaining their original 12th-century layout and alignment, while new structures, built under a contract drawn up in 1378, were grafted onto them.

It is also possible to see from here how well defended the approaches to the gatehouse were. The moat was originally covered by a drawbridge, which like the one in front of the inner gatehouse could be raised to stand upright against a timber framework, in that position constituting a first barrier against further progress towards the gate passage behind. The barbican above provided a vantage point from which to fire missiles at attackers. Behind the barbican is the portcullis, which can still be seen hanging above the grooves in which it slid up and down. Then came the gates, essentially the reinforced oak ones visible today. Despite some repairs, they have preserved most of their original timber and ironwork. The wicket in the eastern gate enabled people to come and go when the gates were closed at night. Another pair of gates closed the passage at the far end.

Looking in the opposite direction, there are walls extending south from the castle's curtain walls. The little tower on the west side is the Tile Tower, so-called from an old word for brick. It was built by the future King Richard III, whose coat of arms was once on a plaque on its outside wall. These walls were once connected directly to the city walls of Carlisle, making city and castle a single, huge defensive system, with the city as its outworks and the castle the place of last resort.

Left: Massive 16th-century buttresses built against the exterior of the inner ward's east wall. These buttresses were needed to support the heavy weight of this thick wall

Below: Engraving of the west walls of the castle and city of Carlisle in 1745, after a watercolour by William Henry Nutter (1819–72). It shows the damage inflicted by the duke of Cumberland's guns when the castle was recovered from the Jacobites, and also demonstrates how the castle and city walls were still linked at this time

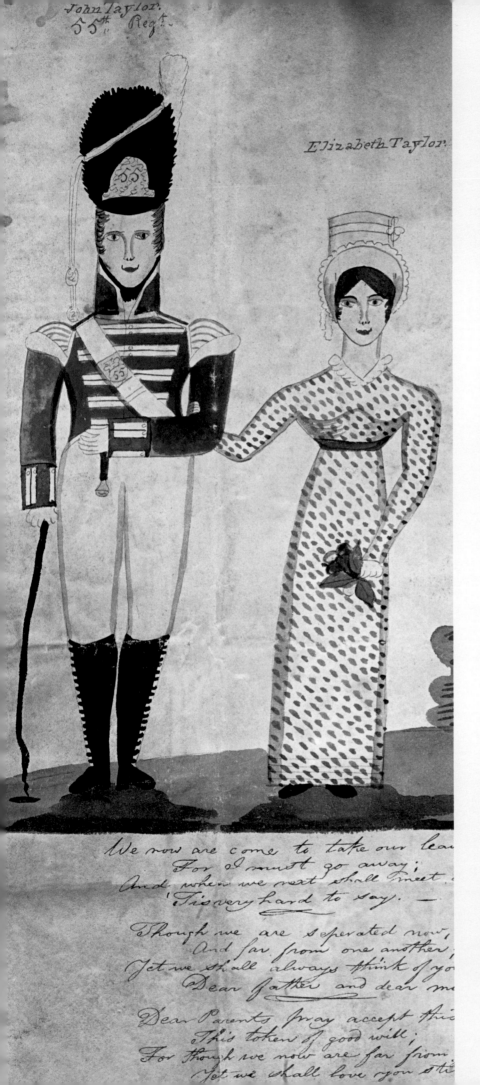

History

Carlisle castle has a rich and dramatic history. The early castle, erected in 1092 by King William Rufus (1087–1100), was probably a largely wooden structure. It was replaced in stone in the early 12th century by King Henry I of England (1100–35) and King David I of Scotland (1124–53). In 1315, it was besieged by the Scots, heralding centuries of border conflict. In the 16th century Mary, queen of Scots, was imprisoned at Carlisle, and in the 1650s the castle was garrisoned by the Commonwealth government. In 1745, it was once more besieged during the Jacobite rebellion, but by the 19th century times were more peaceful, and the castle became a military depot – a role it still serves today.

Left: Illustrated letter showing Private John Taylor, Grenadier Company 55th Foot, and his wife Elizabeth. Produced in 1820 by an unknown artist, the rhyming letter was sent home to Private Taylor's parents. It is now on display in the Border Regiment Museum

EARLY HISTORY

Carlisle has been a military centre for the best part of 2,000 years, thanks to its strategic position at the junction of three rivers and the meeting place of roads north into Scotland and east across the Pennines. In the last quarter of the first century AD, a large Roman fort was established here, on the site of the later castle; this later provided support for the garrisons on Hadrian's Wall and acted as a staging post for troops invading Scotland.

The fort in turn became the nucleus for a prosperous town, named Luguvalium, which existed primarily to serve the garrison. The reuse of part of a third-century altarpiece as a lintel in the outer gatehouse (see pages 6 and 7) bears visible witness to the lengthy Roman occupation of this town, which only ended around the end of the fourth century. The site was then probably occupied by native Britons for over 100 years.

Its fortunes thereafter are often obscure, but in 685 Carlisle is known to have been the centre of a Northumbrian royal estate. In that year St Cuthbert visited the town, where he had been granted estates and founded a nunnery, and was shown round the still-standing Roman walls by the king's reeve, and admired a remarkable fountain that had been built into them.

First Accounts of the Castle

Overrun by Vikings in the late ninth century, 200 years later Carlisle was disputed territory between the kings of England and Scotland. So uncertain was its allegiance that in the year 1092, when the king, William Rufus, set about fixing the borders of the two realms, it was ruled by a man named Dolfin. Even though Dolfin's father was probably the English earl of Northumbria, he might have regarded himself as the vassal of the king of the Scots.

The Anglo-Saxon Chronicle records what happened: 'In this year King William went north to Carlisle with great levies and restored the town, and built the castle. He drove out Dolfin, who had formerly ruled that district, and garrisoned the castle with his men. Thereafter he returned hither southwards, sending very many peasants thither with their wives and livestock to settle there, and till the soil.' Although it is not known exactly

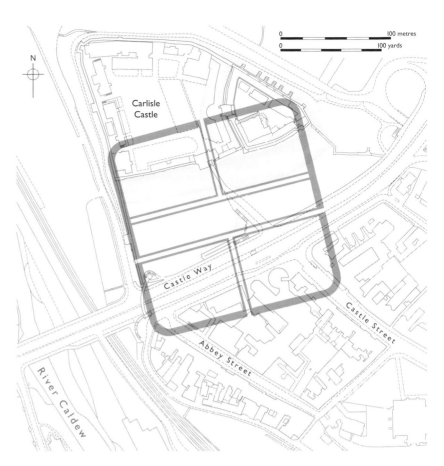

Above: Location of the Roman fort at Carlisle, part of which overlaps with the site of the castle

Left: St Cuthbert with Formenburg, the widow of King Ecgfrith of Northumbria (670–85). The saint visited Carlisle in 685, where he inspected the town's Roman remains and foresaw the death of Ecgfrith, who was defeated and killed in that year by the Picts. From a late 12th century manuscript of the life of St Cuthbert by the Venerable Bede

Right: King David I of Scotland, who took possession of Carlisle in 1135 and probably completed the keep, and his grandson and successor King Malcolm IV (1153–65), who was forced to return Carlisle to English rule in 1157. Manuscript illumination from Malcolm's charter for Kelso Abbey, probably of 1159

Below: King William Rufus enthroned and holding a sword, from the Chronicle of Abingdon, c.1220. Rufus was a famous soldier, and his conquest of Cumberland and occupation of Carlisle was one of the most important achievements of his reign

where this first castle was, it was probably erected where the present castle stands, overlooking the flood plain of the river Eden. Its form might well have been a ringwork of earth, topped by a stockade, with wooden buildings inside.

William Rufus was acting in a hurry in 1092, for fear of Scottish counter-attack. That was still a threat 30 years later. In 1122 Henry I, Rufus's younger brother, came to Carlisle on a tour of inspection of the North, and ordered that it be 'fortified with a castle and towers' – stone defences for the castle and also for the town.

The Construction of the Keep

This meant the beginning of the keep, a mighty symbol of royal lordship, English and then Scottish, for in 1135, following Henry's death, David I, king of Scots, occupied Carlisle by a trick. A supporter of Henry's daughter Matilda against her cousin Stephen, he exploited English difficulties to incorporate much of northern England into his own realm. Scottish chronicles record David as building at Carlisle. Building in stone was a slow process, and very probably he completed

what Henry I had begun. Carlisle became one of the centres from which David ruled his expanded kingdom, until he died in the castle in 1153.

The Withdrawal of the Scots

David's heir, his young grandson King Malcolm IV, was no match in power for King Henry II of England (1154–89), who after his accession in 1154 had the resources of a revived English kingship and half of France at his back. In 1157 the Scots withdrew from Carlisle, and Henry then ordered a substantial reorganization and strengthening of the castle, which acquired a new outer gatehouse, while the spaces behind it were divided into outer and inner wards, the latter now also having its own gatehouse.

This expenditure proved its worth between 1173 and 1174, when the Scottish king William the Lion attempted to take advantage of a widespread rebellion against Henry II to recover what his brother Malcolm IV had lost. Twice he attacked Carlisle with large forces – his counsellors recommended that he threaten to

Left: King Henry II. After recovering Carlisle from Scottish control he financed substantial alterations to the castle. Tomb effigy at Fontevrault Abbey, Maine-et-Loire, France

have the English sheriff, Robert de Vaux, thrown from 'the great ancient tower'. However, despite some hard fighting and an extended siege, which led to the defenders promising to surrender if relief did not come within an agreed period (a conventional and acceptable way of curtailing hostilities), the city and castle held out, until the war was ended by William's defeat and capture at Alnwick.

In 1186 Henry himself came to Carlisle, and his visit led to further works being undertaken in the castle, above all the beginnings of the 'palace' along the north wall of the inner ward. First to be built was a chamber for the king, accompanied by a little tower. A chapel, embellished with panelling and glass windows, followed soon afterwards.

The Capture of Carlisle

The principal beneficiary of the new buildings was King John (1199–1216), who stayed four times in Carlisle and spent much money on the castle, which became one of the bases from which he and his followers oppressed the north of England. As resentment bred resistance and finally outright

rebellion, the English barons made an alliance with the Scottish king Alexander II, whereupon in 1216 the citizens of Carlisle surrendered their city to the latter without even attempting to resist.

The castle held out, and was captured through a methodical siege, one of the few such captures in its history. The south curtain was sapped by miners while the outer gatehouse was bombarded with missiles so heavily that it was still 'cracked from top to bottom' 40 years later. Then, once the attackers were inside the outer ward, the inner gatehouse, too, was shelled into submission and left badly damaged.

King John died in October 1216, and the Scots withdrew from Carlisle soon afterwards. The Treaty of York in 1237, whereby they abandoned their claims to the northern counties of England, should have meant that Carlisle was no longer in danger of attack from the north, and indeed, for much of the 13th century peace prevailed in the borders. As a result the castle was neglected, and a report in 1256 makes dismal reading, with building after building 'very greatly in need of repairing and roofing'.

EDWARD I AND THE SCOTTISH WARS

Things changed abruptly in 1296, when centuries of Anglo-Scottish conflict began, resulting from the determination of King Edward I (1272–1307), fresh from the conquest of Wales, to rule the Scots as well. Carlisle, some seven miles from the border, was in a dangerously exposed position, and the castle became a command centre both for the defence of north-west England and for operations in Scotland. Edward himself came to Carlisle several times, making a last visit of nearly three months at the end of his life in 1307. He stayed in the priory, beside the cathedral, while the castle was occupied by his second wife, Queen Margaret, who no doubt stayed in the 'palace', where a bath was installed for her. More substantial works included a stone tower in the

south-east corner of the inner ward that eventually came to be known as Queen Mary's Tower. Probably Edward died believing that his successors would be staying regularly in Carlisle, on their way to visit conquered Scotland.

CARLISLE UNDER SIEGE, 1315

It did not work out like that. Edward II's military incompetence and political folly led to a remarkable reversal of fortunes. The Scots drove out the invaders and then turned on northern England with devastating effect. In 1314 they routed a huge English army at Bannockburn, and in July 1315, led by King Robert Bruce, they launched a determined attack on Carlisle. They had brought a siege engine, which was set up outside the city's west wall, just below the castle.

Right: Miniature showing King Edward I with his clerks and members of his court, late 13th century. Although the king himself stayed in the priory at Carlisle during the royal visit of 1307, his wife Queen Margaret stayed in the castle, where a chapel and a bath were installed for her use

The Rise and Fall of Andrew Harclay

The commander of the defences of Carlisle in 1315 was Sir Andrew Harclay, sheriff of Cumberland since 1312 and an experienced soldier. He was clearly a man who led from the front – a contemporary drawing of the siege shows him leaning over the battlements, identifiable both by his coat of arms and by the huge crest of feathers in his helmet, and hurling a spear through a luckless Scot below. He reached the peak of his career in 1322, when he led a force of northerners into Yorkshire to intercept and defeat the king's baronial enemies at Boroughbridge, for which a grateful Edward II rewarded him by making him earl of Carlisle. It was an astonishing promotion for the son of a Westmorland knight. Early in January 1323, however, without royal authority, he concluded a treaty with King Robert recognizing Scottish independence, as the only way to end the fighting and destruction. His plans were betrayed to Edward, and on 25 February a small group of loyalists – men he trusted but who probably resented his sudden rise – surprised Harclay in Carlisle Castle and arrested him. Sentenced to a traitor's death, he was dragged on a hurdle to the gallows on Harraby Hill outside the city, where he was hanged and his body quartered. With his last breath he proclaimed his good intentions in negotiating with the Scots. His head was set on London Bridge, one of his quarters on Carlisle Castle keep. Only five years later was his sister allowed to gather his remains for Christian burial.

Sentenced to a traitor's death, Harclay was hanged and his body quartered. With his last breath, he proclaimed his good intentions in negotiating with the Scots

But it did little good, nor did repeated efforts to scale the walls achieve anything.

For one thing the English were ready for them. There was a garrison of between 400 and 500 men, reinforced by the townsmen. The gates had been blocked, the houses outside the walls demolished to give the garrison a clear field of fire. The walls were lined with missile-throwing engines. But no less important was the weather. 1315 was a year of endless rain, which ruined harvests all over Europe. At Carlisle it turned the approaches to the walls into a quagmire. The mobile tower that the Scots planned to wheel up to the walls stuck fast in the mud before it got near them. The moats outside the walls were so full of water that it proved impossible either to fill or to bridge them. All attempts at mining were quickly flooded. For 11 days the Scots persisted, but to no avail. A last desperate attempt to storm the walls was beaten off, and on 1 August they withdrew, leaving their stone-thrower behind. Only two Englishmen were killed during the siege.

Right: A castle facing bombardment by a cannon and mortar, firing stone missiles. In this illumination, from a late 15th-century Flemish chronicle, it is only the attackers who have guns; at Carlisle, however, there were six cannon like this one in the castle by 1430

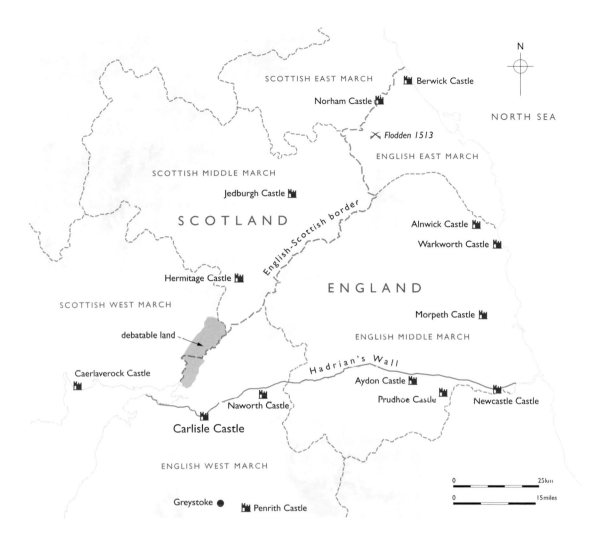

Left: A map of the English and Scottish Marches in the 16th century, showing the area of debatable land on the border and the high concentration of castles just south of Hadrian's Wall

THE AGE OF THE MARCH WARDENS: PERCYS, NEVILLES AND DACRES

The kings of England refused to renounce their claims to rule over Scotland, and the wars continued. Often hostilities were confined to harassing raids and cattle-stealing, but sometimes they involved large-scale invasions by substantial armies. The 1370s and 1380s were a particularly violent period, which saw Scottish forces make a number of attacks deep into north-west England. It was this crisis that led to the rebuilding of the castle's outer gatehouse, and also to the first appearance of guns. Two were recorded in 1380, and three more in 1384, two of them set on the keep and the third at the north-west angle of the outer ward. These early examples of artillery were made of brass, but by 1430 the castle held six cannon, made of longer-lasting iron.

The increasing militarization of the borders impoverished peasants and farmers, but brought wealth to the March wardens who were the crown's principal officers on the borders, responsible as such for regional defence. In times of relative peace the office could be entrusted to the bishop of Carlisle (in 1366 Bishop Thomas Appleby even used his position to grant a safe conduct to Scots wishing to attend Carlisle fair), but in periods of open warfare experienced soldiers were required, and the wardens became increasingly likely to be great lords, men of power in the north. When Percys and Nevilles held the wardenship, the crown paid them large salaries which they then used to pay troops of their own retainers, so effectively maintaining private armies at the king's expense. Henry Percy, known as 'Hotspur', and later Richard Neville, earl of Warwick, 'the Kingmaker', were both at various times wardens of the West March. When such men fell out with their paymasters, their private resources, reinforced by royal money, made them highly dangerous, and each was eventually killed in rebellion against the Crown. Edward IV made sure of having a loyal warden by appointing his own brother, Richard, duke of Gloucester, later King Richard III (1483–5).

Under King Henry VII (1485–1509) the warden's wings were clipped. Instead of appointing a great noble, the cautious king appointed a local baron, with a greatly reduced salary. Thomas, Lord Dacre, was the dominant force in the West March for 40 years, to the extent that many thought him too powerful in the North. His son William, who was intermittently warden of the March during the 40 years following his father's death in 1525, was also regarded with considerable suspicion at Westminster, particularly for his contacts with Scotland, which in 1534 justified his being arrested and charged with treason. Uniquely in the reign of King Henry VIII (1509–47) he was acquitted, but held no Crown office for 15 years. Recovering the wardenship in 1549, William was hampered by local rivalries, and sometimes also by his staunch Catholicism. Nevertheless he lived splendidly, maintaining a magnificent household and surrounding himself with loyal and warlike retainers. It is not surprising that shortly before William's death in 1563 the bishop of Carlisle should have described him as 'something too mighty in this country and as it were a prince.'

Thomas, Lord Dacre

Thomas Dacre was a fine if sometimes impetuous soldier, who did good service at the battle of Flodden in 1513, and earned the hatred of the Scots for discovering the body of King James IV afterwards, so proving that he was dead. His inheritance of the baronies of Burgh-by-Sands and Gilsland, up against the border with Scotland, made him rich only in men, in the number of tenants he could call out to fight for him (4,000 on one occasion). He became rich not through his wardenship but by eloping with the heiress to the barony of Greystoke, which enabled him to live in fine style in castles at Naworth, a few miles north-east of Carlisle, and Morpeth in Northumberland. Visitors to the latter commented on his fine plate and the fashionable tapestries on the walls. Intelligent and cultivated, he was also a talented diplomat, who became a familiar figure at the Scottish court and co-operated with King James against border robbers ('reivers') – the two men played cards in intervals between hanging thieves. His skills, experience and local resources made Dacre indispensable in the government of the North, so that he became warden not only of the West March but of the East and Middle Marches as well. But the additional responsibility proved too much for him, and by the time he died in 1525, by falling from his horse, he was in disgrace for failing to keep the peace on the borders.

Above right: Angel with a shield bearing the arms of the Dacre and Vaux families, set within the Garter. Detail from a watercolour drawing by Peter Dunn of the south face of the tomb at Lanercost Priory of Thomas, second Lord Dacre, who was made a knight of the Garter in 1518 (see picture on facing page)
Right: King Richard III by an unknown artist, late 16th century (after a late 15th-century original)

RICARDVS . III . ANG . REX .

THE SIXTEENTH-CENTURY CASTLE

Neither the early Tudor kings nor the Dacres spent much money on Carlisle Castle, which rapidly became dangerously dilapidated. A report of 1529 described a complex in which practically every building was on the verge of collapse. The very gates at the entrance were 'clean consumed and gone', the castle guns were 'of small effect and litill in value', and roof after roof was 'clene gone down', while the lead roof of the keep was 'broken and consumed'. It was the rising of 1536–7 against Henry VIII, known as the Pilgrimage of Grace, during which Carlisle was attacked by rebels, and then fears of attack by Scots in alliance with France, that led to the castle being overhauled. In 1541 the task was entrusted to a Moravian land surveyor, Stephan von Haschenperg, who had already worked on England's south-coast defences. His task was to modernize the defences of Carlisle by equipping them both to face and to carry heavy guns, and to that end he oversaw the making of bulwarks outside the castle's east curtain, the construction of the half-moon battery in the outer ward, and the strengthening of the inner ward's wall-walk and the roof of the keep to enable them to bear the weight of cannon. He was also responsible for the construction of the citadel at the city's south gate. The works went on slowly, and the government soon began to wonder if it was getting value for money. Haschenperg quarrelled with his superiors, and was finally dismissed in 1543, having 'spent great treasure to no purpose'. By this time it was probably clear that Carlisle was no longer in serious danger of attack, and that as a place of defence the castle was becoming something of a white elephant. It remained useful as a base from which to supervise the still unruly borders, and as a lock-up to hold cattle thieves. But even in that capacity it was vulnerable. A late 16th-century exchequer record lists a payment for 'the repairing and amending of the postern gate which William of Kynmowth did break under when he stole away'. Such is the official record of the escape of the reiver 'Kinmont Willie' – William Armstrong of Kinmont – who was rescued from the castle by a band of Scots on the night of 13 April 1596. An exciting border ballad has made this one of the best-known episodes in Carlisle's history, disguising the extent to which the rescuers had inside help, and the fact that, far from being chained down in a dungeon, Armstrong was detained in an easily accessible building in the outer ward.

Above: *The dolphin, one of four heraldic beasts (bull, dolphin, griffin and ram) carved from a single oak tree in the early 16th century. It was the emblem of Elizabeth Greystoke, the wife of Thomas, second Lord Dacre. Once housed in the hall of Naworth Castle, the beasts, which are just over 2 metres (almost 7 feet) tall, can now be seen at the Victoria and Albert Museum, London*
Left: *The south face of the tomb of Thomas, second Lord Dacre, at Lanercost Priory. Both sides are carved with coats of arms illustrating the ancestry and connections of his family*

Right: Bird's-eye map of
Carlisle in about 1560, by an
unknown artist, showing how
the castle, at the top, and
the city were enclosed within
a continuous sequence of
walls, making them a single
defensive unit

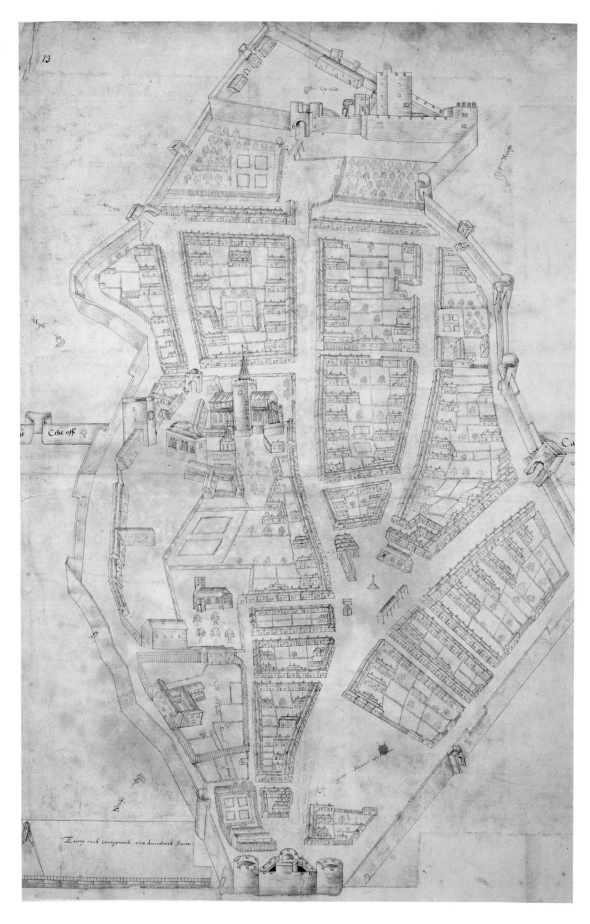

THE STUARTS AND THE CIVIL WAR

Mary, queen of Scots (see pages 12 and 13), was executed in 1587. Sixteen years later, in 1603, her son King James VI of Scotland became James I of England (1603–25). In 1617, on his way back from a visit to his homeland, James visited Carlisle and stayed in the castle. He found it in a bad way, but did nothing to restore it, and in 1633 most of its guns were removed. The union of the English and Scottish Crowns had brought peace to the borders, and should have made Carlisle Castle completely obsolete. But religious differences, and the authoritarian and insensitive rule of King Charles I (1625–49), provoked discontent that became armed resistance, first in Scotland and then in England as well. Civil war between king and Parliament broke out in 1642. As tensions mounted, Carlisle, as 'a place of great importance', was put in a state of defence, and three batteries of guns were set up in the castle, at the north-west and south-west corners of the outer ward and on the inner ward's east-facing wall. But the attack thus prepared for was a long time coming.

Occupied by cavalier forces, Carlisle played little part in the Civil War until the battle of Marston Moor, on 2 July 1644, gave control of most of northern England to Parliament and the Scots. It was the latter who, in the following October, put Carlisle under siege, surrounding the city with guns and earthworks. They did not risk an all-out assault, but settled down to starve the city out, confining their military operations to occasional cannonades and cavalry skirmishes with any members of the garrison who ventured out.

In the spring of 1645 English troops reinforced the besiegers, who tightened their grip on Carlisle. Inside the city, money to pay the soldiers had to be struck from plate commandeered from the townsfolk, and food ran desperately short. All the horses were eaten, then any dogs and rats that could be found. Finally, on 25 June, three weeks after the cavalier defeat at Naseby ended any remaining hope of relief, the city surrendered, and the victors entered Carlisle, described shortly afterwards as 'the model of misery and desolation'. A number of old buildings that formed part of the Carlisle Priory complex were pulled down and their masonry reused to repair damage done to the castle during the siege.

Carlisle Castle was garrisoned under both the Commonwealth (when cannon were put on top of the keep) and the Restoration monarchy. But it was not regarded by either regime as a stronghold of major importance – when a report of 1661 recommended spending nearly £2,500 on works, the government provided just £200. The guns were used only to salute royal birthdays and important visitors, and by the end of the 17th century the garrison had been withdrawn.

THE EIGHTEENTH CENTURY

The first Jacobite rebellion of 1715, by supporters of the exiled Stuarts against the newly installed Hanoverian monarchy, made little impact, though afterwards prisoners were held in the two gatehouses and the keep – two escaped and the rest were pardoned. In the 1720s and 1730s the castle was manned, after a fashion, by a company of veterans, who lived in the city and spent most of their time fishing. When the governor of Carlisle, the commanding officer of the city's defences, made a visit of inspection in 1739, he was warned not to walk along the wall joining the city to the castle, 'for fear it should break down'.

Above: Coins struck in 1645 from plate commandeered from the townspeople of Carlisle, when the city was besieged by Scots and parliamentarians during the Civil War. The people of Carlisle were forced to eat horses, rats and dogs during the siege
Left: James I painted in c.1610 by John de Critz. The king visited Carlisle Castle in 1617

THE JACOBITE REBELLION OF 1745

The Jacobite rebellion of 1745, led by King James II's grandson Charles Edward Stuart (1720–88), came as a shock to the peaceful military backwater that was Carlisle. By September it was clear that a Scottish invasion might be imminent, and the local militia was called out to safeguard the city and castle. But even with the assistance of able-bodied townsmen, Colonel James Durand, whom the government had sent to take command, found that a force of about 1,250 men was nowhere near enough to defend the city against perhaps 5,000 Scots. To make matters worse, as the Jacobites approached Carlisle early in November, the principal Hanoverian army at Newcastle was prevented from crossing the Pennines by heavy snow. On 9 November the invaders drew up outside the city, where morale plummeted at the prospect of imminent attack by bloodthirsty savages – for such was the reputation of the Highlanders. Men began to desert, and on 14 November the mayor and corporation of Carlisle decided to capitulate. Durand wanted to retire into the castle and hold out there, but the Jacobites refused to accept the city's surrender without that of the castle, and with too few men to have any hope of effective resistance behind walls described as 'very old, thin, and decayed', Durand had to surrender. On 17 November Charles Edward Stuart entered the city, according to tradition preceded by 100 pipers.

The Jacobites had very little support in Carlisle and Cumberland, and when their main army marched on south, leaving a garrison in the castle, a group of townsmen conspired to seize it for King George II (1714–60). The plot was discovered, but the failure mattered little, for the Scottish army soon returned, and on

Right: Plan (c.1746) of the siege of Carlisle by the duke of Cumberland's army on 21 December 1745. Following the siege, many Jacobite soldiers were imprisoned in Carlisle Castle, and nine were executed on 18 October 1746. The event attracted a large crowd, but afterwards 'many returned home with full resolution to see no more of the kind, it was so shocking'

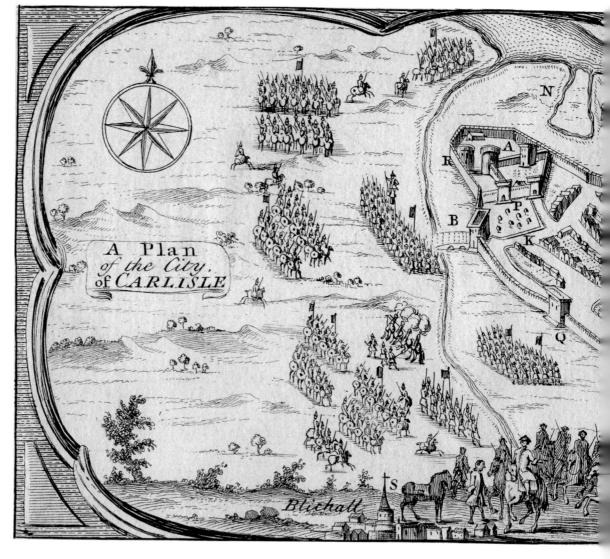

20 December retreated across the border, leaving some 400 men to hold off the English pursuit, led by the duke of Cumberland. Carlisle was surrounded once more, and siege guns from Whitehaven and mortars from Newcastle soon launched a bombardment which neither the city nor the castle – contemptuously described by Cumberland as 'an old hen-coop' – was equipped to resist. Holes were blasted in the walls, one of them just below the castle's west curtain, until on 30 December the Jacobites surrendered.

Cumberland hastened north, to overwhelm the Scots at Culloden on the following 16 April, and Carlisle Castle, having been once more used as a prison for captured Jacobites – at least 31 were hanged this time, though most were transported to North America – fell back into its accustomed somnolence. It remained in use as a military store, but by the end of the 18th century

Left: Charles Edward Stuart, 'Bonnie Prince Charlie', who captured Carlisle in 1745, by Maurice Quentin de la Tour, 1748

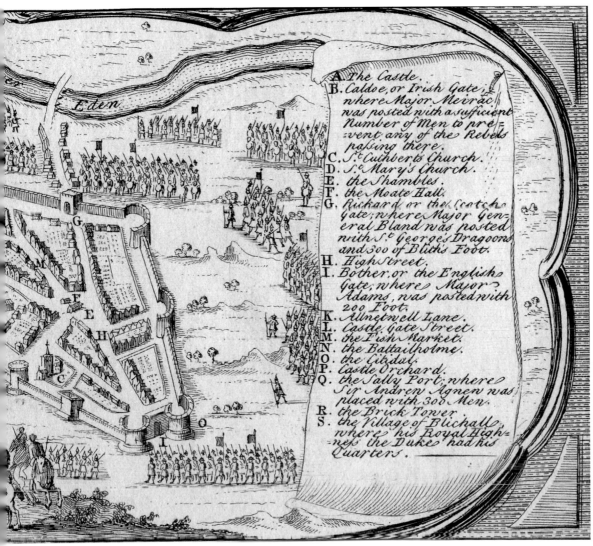

Eden

A. The Castle.
B. Caldoe, or Irish Gate, where Major Meirac was posted with a sufficient Number of Men to prevent any of the Rebels passing there.
C. St Cuthbert's Church.
D. St Mary's Church.
E. the Shambles.
F. the Moate Hall.
G. Rickard or the Scotch Gate, where Major General Bland was posted with St George's Dragoons and 300 of Blith's Foot.
H. High Street.
I. Bother, or the English Gate, where Major Adams, was posted with 200 Foot.
K. Allnetwell Lane.
L. Castle Gate Street.
M. the Fish Market.
N. the Battailholme.
O. the Citadal.
P. Castle Orchard.
Q. the Sally Port, where Sir Andrew Agnew was placed with 300 Men.
R. the Brick Tower.
S. the Village of Blichall, where his Royal Highness the Duke had his Quarters.

Right: Cummersdale Mill, Carlisle, painted in about 1844 by Samuel Bough (1822–78). Cummersdale was one of four spinning mills at Carlisle, reflecting the importance of the city's textile industry. The textile workers campaigned for political reform

Bottom right: Cartoon attributed to George Cruikshank (1792–1878), showing the 'Peterloo' massacre of 1819, when 11 people attending a reform meeting in St Peter's Fields, Manchester, were killed by the Manchester Yeomanry. Fears of similar disorder at Carlisle led to the castle being once more manned by regular soldiers

was increasingly valued as a tourist attraction, especially for the views from the top of the keep. 'The prospect from the great tower is noble', as one visitor put it.

RADICALS AND CHARTISTS

It was the French Revolution, and the encouragement that it gave to British radicals, especially in newly developing manufacturing towns, that saved Carlisle Castle from becoming a picturesque ruin. By the late 18th century Carlisle was a major centre of the textile industry, and its weavers, in particular, were vociferous campaigners for political reform. Although an alarmed government responded by building barracks for troops all over the country, Carlisle Castle was at first used only as a depot for arms, holding thousands of muskets, while soldiers were billeted on the townspeople.

In spite of occasional outbreaks of disorder, this remained the situation until October 1819, when fears that radical extremists would storm the castle to seize the guns inside led to its being put in a state of defence. Troops were brought in to man the walls, from where they watched protesters marching with banners carrying mottoes such as 'Trial by Jury' and 'Liberty or

Death'. Such was the apparent threat to public order that it was decided that Carlisle Castle must be converted into barracks, and occupied by soldiers on a permanent basis.

From the 1820s onwards, old buildings were remodelled and new ones put up to house troops. In 1826 the process began of levelling the parade ground and gravelling it over, quickly followed by the filling up of the ditch in front of the half-moon battery (whose upper levels were demolished in 1835). In 1827 the armoury in the outer ward was converted into barracks for 114 men, and in 1836 a new block was erected nearby for some 70 more soldiers. Meanwhile all

Life in the Early Victorian Castle

When Lieutenant Crowther's mistress came to see him, Gunner Hudson's wife would bang on the ceiling to let him know she had arrived

The report of a court martial in 1849 provides a vivid picture of life in the castle at this time. Lieutenant Crowther of the 63rd Regiment of Foot was charged with attempting to steal the keys to the mess-room cupboard from one of the soldiers. As an officer he lived upstairs in what was left of the 'palace' in the Inner ward, in quarters reached by a complicated network of stairs and passages. There and everywhere else the castle teemed with people. Not only were there 239 soldiers in the castle, but some of them had wives and children with them, and many – privates as well as officers – had servants, too. Crowther had two servants, one of whom, an Indian named Yagrahambome, had come back with him from service in the East. Life

for all was fairly comfortless. The only lighting came from candles, and water had to be fetched in jugs from the yard. Bugle-calls marked the passage of time. Bored soldiers took to drink – two men were said to be 'in liquor five days out of seven' – others went out 'over the barrack wall'. Crowther himself was keeping a mistress, a local dressmaker called Jane Macleod, and when she came to see him, Gunner Hudson's wife, who worked in the kitchen downstairs, would either bang on the ceiling with a broomstick or send her young son up to let Crowther know that his lady friend had arrived. The court learnt about Jane with equanimity, but found Crowther guilty as charged and dismissed him from the army.

Right: Watercolour by William Henry Nutter (1819–72) showing the view out of the gateway in 1835, with a soldier of the 34th Regiment. The gates themselves, and the portcullis above them, look much as they do today, but city houses press closely against the south face of the castle. The cathedral tower can be seen in the distance

Above: Border Regiment
recruitment poster, 1922.
Carlisle Castle was a centre
of army recruitment from
the late 19th century

MODERN TIMES

When Lieutenant Crowther was cashiered the social tensions that had brought him and his regiment to Carlisle were beginning to ease. The castle remained in military occupation, but became primarily a training depot and recruiting centre, especially after a major reorganization between 1872 and 1873, when the 34th Cumberland and 55th Westmorland Regiments took up residence. In 1881 they were amalgamated to form the Border Regiment. Conditions for the men slowly improved. Proper sewerage and drainage made the castle healthier; the hospital – described in a report of 1859 as 'one of the worst army hospitals we have inspected' – was greatly enlarged. The medieval buildings in the inner ward became storehouses, and more space was created for soldiers by enlarging the old canteen and turning it into barracks, with a recreation room and reading room as well. Married quarters were built just outside the walls.

By the end of the 19th century Carlisle Castle was increasingly appreciated as an ancient monument, and professional guides – often highly unreliable, even though they were sometimes retired soldiers – showed visitors round. The War Office began to consult the Office of Works – the forerunner of English Heritage – when it wanted to make alterations. In 1911 the two departments made an agreement, dividing responsibility for the castle's future development. The arrangements worked well. During the First World War the castle was used mainly to train recruits, and they probably provided the labour force when the lower levels of the half-moon battery, and the ditch in front, were excavated between 1917 and 1919. The Office of Works, for its part, made no objection when a new regimental institute was erected in the outer ward, opening in 1932.

During the Second World War an anti-aircraft gun was set up on top of the keep, and even then the formalities were observed, and the Office of Works was asked for, and gave, its consent, on condition that nothing was done to damage the roof. In the years after 1945 these arrangements remained in force, until in 1959 the regimental depot was closed. But the armed services retain a presence, and keep up the centuries-old tradition of military occupation; the

the medieval buildings had men packed into them, and in 1839 there were nearly 250 men in the castle. By then a new movement for political reform had arisen, known as Chartism from the 'People's Charter' containing its programme, and quickly won support. In October 1838 a mass meeting was held on Carlisle Sands, with banners and brass bands, and 50 years later old men could still remember the 'perfectly furious' applause that greeted attacks on the government.

Hauling Down the Flag

When you were posted to Carlisle Castle you quickly became aware of the history of the regiment, and you realized that others shared your feelings

Colonel Ralph May (1927–2012) remembered Carlisle Castle in its last days of military occupation:

'As you entered the castle, there was a regimental policeman on the gate. Behind him was the guard room with the provost sergeant and the duty drummer whose bugle calls timed the routine of the day. The square was normally occupied by drill squads, watched by members of the public, who were also allowed into the inner ward and the keep, where the regimental museum was housed.

'The depot's task was to train recruits. At any one time there were three platoons of them, living in Ypres and Gallipoli blocks. The officers, NCOs and other members of staff were dotted all over the castle. Every eight weeks there was an intake of recruits, with a passing out parade eight weeks later, when a band played and some local dignitary or distinguished officer took the salute. The depot was very much a part of city and county life. Soldiers took part in Remembrance Sunday parades and other ceremonies, and helped to provide a guard of honour when royalty visited Cumbria. Now and then recruiting marches were staged in local towns, perhaps accompanied by the regimental band.

'When you were posted to Carlisle Castle you quickly became aware of the history of the regiment, and you realized that others shared your feelings. In 1959 it was decided that the Border Regiment should merge with the King's Own Royal Regiment, to become the King's Own Royal Border Regiment, while the depot was to close. When the news broke, the depot arranged a march through the counties of Cumberland and Westmorland. Thousands turned out to see and cheer the Border Regiment as it made a last parade in its home territory. Finally, on 1 October, not long after the last passing out parade, came the sad moment when the regimental flag was lowered for the last time. By the end of the month the last regular soldier had gone, leaving two retired officers to look after the regiment's affairs, and the museum in the inner ward as a lasting memorial to old glories.'

Right: Colonel Ralph May lowers the flag of the Border Regiment for the last time on 1 October 1959, when the regiment became part of the new King's Own Royal Border Regiment. An NCO can be seen in the background lowering the flag over the gatehouse at the same time

Right: Field Marshall Montgomery leaves Carlisle Castle in his famous Humber staff car, having received the freedom of the city, 17 May 1947

territorial army and the army cadet force still have bases here, while the King's Own Royal Border Regiment, now part of the Duke of Lancaster's Regiment, not only maintains a museum in the castle but also occupies the Victorian officers' mess as its regimental HQ.

The various changes to its use in the 19th and 20th centuries did not make the castle any less important in the life of Carlisle. Valued as a source of employment and a tourist attraction, its historic interest and associations also evoked considerable local pride. The city's identification with the castle was increasingly extended to the Border Regiment that was now permanently stationed within it. In the words of the mayor, speaking after dinner in the sergeants' mess in April 1936, 'the name of Carlisle was synonymous with the Regiment'. In keeping with this attitude, great efforts were made over many years to ensure that the castle was seen to best advantage, by demolishing buildings in front of it and ensuring that no more were put up there. This campaign to provide a clear view of the castle from the south was initiated in the city but increasingly had the military's support. In the mid-1870s the War Office had plans to construct

quarters for married soldiers on the gardens in front of the castle; these were successfully resisted by the corporation, which hoped to create 'a magnificent boulevard which will sweep in a grand curve round our ancient castle'. Similar proposals were opposed with equal success in 1891. Later that year the erection of a new red-brick chimney stack against the east side of the keep was denounced in the *Carlisle Journal* as 'the biggest atrocity yet built in Carlisle'. The War Office explained that the chimney was needed for the tailor's and armourer's shops at the base of the keep, but nonetheless agreed to modify the colour of the new structure so that it blended in with the neighbouring buildings. By 1925 the corporation had spent over £11,000 in buying up property in order to demolish it and open up the view of the castle, and it spent more money for this purpose afterwards. The busy motorway which now separates the castle physically from the city hinders access and spoils the view that was thus created, but credit should still be given to the cooperation between the townsfolk of Carlisle and the army authorities who together brought these potentially fine vistas into being.